HOPE
AND
LIGHT
FOR
ADVENT

Guided
Reflections

Mark E. Thibodeaux, SJ

the WORD
among us®
press

Published by The Word Among Us Press

7115 Guilford Drive, Suite 100

Frederick, Maryland 21704

wau.org

28 27 26 25 24   1 2 3 4 5

ISBN: 978-1-59325-724-8

eISBN: 978-1-59325-725-5

Design by Rose Audette

Library of Congress Control Number: 2024946115

CONTENTS

Preface

There's a baby coming! What joy these words bring to a young couple wanting to start a family. But with this joy comes anticipation and preparation. There is much that needs to be done in order to create a space—safe, warm, and loving—for this new and tender arrival.

Every Advent, we, too, make this proclamation. There's a baby coming! Christ's coming was not one-and-done. Christ keeps coming into the world. Christ is born again among us . . . and again . . . and again. And for Christ to come again this Christmas, Gabriel is on the move. Gabriel is in search of another womb—another Mary who will answer the call with "Fiat! Let it be done!"

Advent is a season of hope, and my hope for you, gentle reader, is that these reflections might help you to prepare for your own fiat, to create a space within your own "spiritual womb" where Christ might be born again. These reflections will help you make room at your inn. Then Christ indeed will be born again. The Light will come and dispel the darkness, beginning with your own and then brightening every dark corner of a world in ever-greater need of a Prince of Peace, a Wonderful Counselor.

There's a baby coming! Create a space within! Make room!

A Note to the Reader

I make reference to many passages from Scripture in these reflections and so I thought it would be useful to suggest some practical approaches that might help you when you meditate on a passage from or scene in the Bible.

Here's how I proceed when I reflect on a Scripture passage. Let's say my passage that day is from Luke 1:26-38, the Annunciation of the Angel Gabriel to Mary. Before I begin my prayer, I open the Bible to the passage and set it up next to me, right next to my chair. Then I quiet myself until I'm in a place of deep quiet. I usually use some sort of chant or a mantra, saying "Come, Lord Jesus," for example. I continue to say "Come, Lord Jesus, Come, Lord Jesus," but not necessarily out loud. I would most likely say it silently and coordinate my breathing with the words "Come, Lord Jesus"—syncing my breaths in and out with each syllable. What I'm trying to do is get to a deeper state in my soul where I'm starting to sense Christ deep within me. When I get to that very quiet place, I just sit there and rest for a while. I don't pick up the Bible and read the Scripture passage; I just sit and rest.

And then whenever I feel called to, I read the passage aloud. Sometimes I then run the scene in my mind, almost as if I'm watching a television screen. I watch Gabriel come, speak to Mary, and I watch her respond. And then after I watch the scene—maybe I'll watch it a couple of times—I pause and speak with the Lord about what I've seen.

If you follow this approach, then at this point you could tell the Lord the emotions that are stirring in your heart. Observing and reflecting on the scene, you can take note of the emotional movements in your heart, talk about them to the Lord, and then see if you can sense what the Lord is saying back to you.

Another way to do this—and this is a distinctly Ignatian way—is to place yourself inside the scene. So how would that unfold? Well, you imagine yourself to be Mary, for example. You place yourself in the role of Mary and you watch Gabriel come to you, maybe come down from the heavens and speak to you. What does Gabriel look like? St. Ignatius would ask you to get really into the nitty-gritty here. He would want you to describe, for example: Are you, as Mary, sitting on the bed? Are you kneeling on the floor? Or are you outside under a tree? Do you feel the wind on your face? Are you hot or are you cold? What are you seeing? What are you hearing? What are you tasting in the air? What are you smelling? What are your five senses telling you as you're entering into the scene and you're playing the role of Mary? You follow this approach so that you can really be inside that scene. And you play the whole scene forward with you as Mary. You watch yourself say, "May it be done to me."

You do all this two or three times. Then you pull away and speak to God the Father or to Christ the Son about what just happened, about what it was like for you and what was stirring in your heart as you were saying "yes" in the role of Mary. That second phase is called colloquy, a conversation that follows the imaginative exercise using the Scripture passage and the Scripture scene. In the colloquy, you have a conversation with God about all that you've seen and experienced in your meditation. And whether you speak to God the Father or to Christ the Son or even to the Holy Spirit is completely up to you. Whichever Person of the Trinity shows up in your prayer, that's the One you should speak to. You shouldn't force one Person of the Trinity or another—just let whichever One comes to you in your prayer time be the One you speak to in your colloquy.

1

LIGHT IN THE DARKNESS

People sometimes treat the Second Coming of Jesus in a humorous manner. As one bumper sticker says, "Jesus is coming. Look busy!" This is meant as a joke, of course, but all joking aside, some of the readings for Mass during Advent strike a somber tone about his return. We see in the Gospel of Luke, chapter 21, for example, that tribulation will precede his return in glory. Not only will the sun, moon, stars, and nations be dismayed by the roaring of the sea, but people will actually die of fright as they anticipate what's coming upon the world.

Jesus is indeed coming, and he's asking us to be watchful, to "be vigilant" (Luke 21:36). "The heavens will be shaken," he says (21:26). But how does Jesus ask his followers to approach what will undoubtedly be a terrifying time? It seems counterintuitive, but at that moment he wants to find us waiting in joyful, quiet anticipation. He asks that we wait in hope, that we "stand erect and raise [our] heads" (21:28). The Son of Man may come as late as midnight or later than midnight,

During this season of Advent, the Church helps us to reflect on that spiritual experience we know so well: watching and waiting in a pitch-black night.

even at the cock crow in the morning, Jesus says. The Son of Man might come after a long dark night. Nevertheless Scripture assures us that not only will the Son of Man come, but he will come "with power and great glory" (Luke 21:27).

All well and good, we might think. But what about here and now, when we do not see these "signs in the sun, the moon, and the stars," these signifiers of Jesus' return, and yet our own personal world feels shaken? When we are in our own dark night, caught up in fear, perhaps our family in turmoil or our health on the line or our inner world falling apart, and it feels as though the Son of Man is not with us— that we're waiting in the dark and he seems nowhere near? What about those times?

Those times are part of the spiritual life, hard as that might be to accept. But in those turbulent times, Jesus is with us, and we wait for him to reveal his presence to us.

Why is this pertinent in Advent? Because the seasons of our liturgical calendar reflect the seasons of our spiritual life, and the season of Advent is a season of waiting. Think about even such a simple thing as the color of the vestments the priest wears at Mass during Advent. These dark violet vestments signify that we're in a time of penance and preparation—of waiting. That solemn color, however, also indicates that, for each of us, depending on where we are in our spiritual life, waiting will often feel like a dark night of the soul. We feel as if we're lost in the wilderness, it's midnight, and there's no light to be found. Every one of us has endured a moment or a prolonged period when we feel lost in the dark and the light of Christ seems far away. And so during this season of Advent,

We know that God has not gone away, that he is just on the other side of that obstacle—hidden from view but nonetheless fully present to us.

the Church helps us to reflect on that spiritual experience we know so well: watching and waiting in a pitch-black night.

And yet we come to church to profess our faith and also our hope; and the hope that we profess is the reality that Christ is indeed coming—that he's never left us, that he is present, and that even in the darkest of nights, there is a pinpoint of light streaming from a star in the midnight sky. As we light the dark violet Advent candle, this flame—this small flickering flame—signifies our own small flickering hope, even in our darkest night. Because we know that Christ is always with us, even if we can't always sense his presence.

We might ask, in that dark night, as Victor Hugo does in *Les Misérables*,

> Will the future ever arrive? . . . Should we continue to look upwards? Is the light we can see in the sky one of those which will presently be extinguished? The ideal is terrifying to behold, lost as it is in the depth, small, isolated, a pin-point, brilliant but threatened on all sides by the dark forces that surround it; nevertheless, no more in danger than a star in the jaws of the clouds.

As we endure what feels like an unending expanse of blackness, we can be assured that the darkness will not swallow us up. There is a pinpoint of light filled with power and energy, and so we trust.

We come to church professing our faith in that pinpoint of light—we cling to the truth that the jaws of the night will not close in on it. And yet, as the prophet Isaiah says, "You have hidden your face from us" (64:6). We do at times feel this way in our dark night: God has hidden his face from us. But consider the reaction of babies to the game of peek-a-boo.

Child psychologists tell us babies react so dramatically to the peek-a-boo game because when we hide our face, a baby thinks we're completely gone, that we've actually disappeared. When we show our face again, the baby lights up because once again mom or dad is present.

When we feel as though God has hidden his face—that something has obscured God's face—we begin to feel that he's not present anymore. But we know something that babies don't know: we know that God has not gone away, that he is just on the other side of that obstacle—hidden from view but nonetheless fully present to us. We're not babies in the spiritual life—we're not playing peek-a-boo with God. We come to church to profess that even though God's face is obscured at times, God is faithful, he is present, and Christ will come again. The light of Christ will come to the world. Psalm 23 proclaims,

> The LORD is my shepherd,
>   there is nothing I lack.
> In green pastures he makes me lie down;
>   to still waters he leads me;
>   he restores my soul. (23:1-3)

How pleasant, we might be tempted to think. *It sounds like the psalmist is having a very good day.* But actually, if you read the psalm carefully, this person is going through a dark night. He says this: "Even though I walk through the valley of the shadow of death" (Psalm 23:4). *The valley of the shadow of death.* The psalmist is going through a dark night of the soul. But then he says,

> Even though I walk through the valley of the shadow of death,
>> I will fear no evil, for you are with me;
>> your rod and your staff comfort me. . . .
> Indeed, goodness and mercy will pursue me
>> all the days of my life. (23:4, 6)

This poor man is walking through a dark valley, but he knows that goodness and mercy are following behind. "Goodness and kindness shall pursue me," one of the translations says. "Goodness and kindness are coming after me," he tells us. "I know that I'm in darkness now, but goodness and kindness are on the way!"

This is what we profess when we come to church. In Advent, we symbolically sit as a community in the dark night. We sit together in the dark and wait with patience, and with hope as well, knowing that Christ is coming.

The entrance procession as the priest walks down the center aisle at the beginning of Mass is more than a pleasant ritual that we watch while singing the opening hymn. That entrance procession symbolizes Christ walking amid the people. Before you've said even a word of the liturgy, you've made a profession. By standing as the priest walks up the aisle, representing Christ walking by, you are proclaiming that you believe Christ walks beside you.

Even if God's face is obscured for now, let us watch and wait, but let us wait with patience and with hope, knowing that the light of Christ will shine brightly and that goodness and kindness shall follow us all the days of our lives.

FOR REFLECTION

1. Even when you're going through a dark night, God is still present. He has never left you. Meditate on one aspect of his presence and faithfulness today, drawing from Psalm 23. Is it his leading you to waters of rest? Or is it his presence by your side? Spend some time leaning on a verse that speaks to you.

2. We experience Advent as a church community, waiting together in the dark for the coming light. How might you bring light and hope—a listening heart, encouragement, companionship—to someone who is struggling through a period of personal darkness?

2

THE LAMB AND THE LION

The Israelites of Jesus' day thought that the Messiah would come as a military leader—a hero who would gather the Israelite people for a military revolution to overthrow the Romans. You can see why they would have thought that as they listened to the words of Isaiah who prophesied seven hundred years *before* Jesus' time. In 63 BC, however, the Romans occupied Israel, and it is against that background that the Israelites heard the prophet Isaiah say,

> A shoot shall sprout from the stump of Jesse, . . .
> He shall judge the poor with justice,
>   and decide fairly for the land's afflicted.
> He shall strike the ruthless with the rod of his mouth. (11:1, 4)

Who are the ruthless? For the Israelites of Jesus' day, they were the Romans who are occupying their land. What justice? The Messiah was going to correct the injustice of the Roman occupation. "Justice shall be the band around his waist, and

The ruthlessness that the Messiah
wants to root out is actually
inside me.

faithfulness a belt upon his hips," Isaiah continues (11:5). The Messiah, who was just, was going to overthrow the Romans, who were wicked.

Little did they know (but we know) that the idea that some people are entirely bad and some people are purely good is simply not true. The truth is: I am good, but I'm bad, too. I've got a bit of both inside me. I am ruthless and wicked, and I'm also good and gentle. The cutting line between good and bad does not go across peoples or nations or cultures. It splits right through the center of you and of me. The ruthlessness that the Messiah wants to root out is actually inside me. It's not a matter of "those people over there." We deny the truth when we claim that "We're the good ones. They're the bad ones. He's going to tear apart those bad ones." No, *he's got to take the ruthlessness out of me.*

And as he does, as I submit to his pruning, the beautiful lines that are so iconic for us in Advent take on deeper meaning:

> The wolf shall be a guest of the lamb,
>> and the leopard shall lie down with the young goat;
> The calf and the young lion shall browse together, . . .
> The cow and the bear shall graze,
>> together their young shall lie down;
>> the lion shall eat hay like the ox.
>> The baby shall play by the viper's den,
>>> and the child lay his hand on the adder's lair. (Isaiah 11:6-8)

Once I accept that I've got both good and bad inside me, it's easier to accept that I'm the cow, but I'm the bear, too. I'm the lamb, but I'm the wolf, too. I'm the kid, but I'm the leopard, too. And so what we want to pray when we pray about the coming of the Messiah is not that he come and defeat "those people over there." When we pray, we ask him to come and take care of the leopard that's inside of me, the lion that's inside of me, the snake, the adder, the badger inside of me. And notice, by the way, that he doesn't kill them. He doesn't say, "I'm going to come and kill the snake and the adder." He domesticates them; he tames them.

Let's pray, this Advent, that he would come and tame the lion, the adder, and the wolf inside of each of us.

FOR REFLECTION

1. During Advent, our preparations for Christmas sometimes overshadow the truth that the Messiah has come to save us from our sins—from the bear and leopard within. Prepare your heart to bring any failings to God in the Sacrament of Confession this Advent, anticipating the great joy of forgiveness.

2. Consider how God has "tamed" the ruthlessness within you. Thank him for this grace, and invite him to do more work within your heart this Advent.

3

ON THAT DAY, A FEAST

When Christ our Savior comes, he brings abundance with him. It's not simply that he answers our prayers and moves us to a satisfactory position. He brings abundance. Isaiah tells us that when the Messiah—the Savior—comes, he will set a feast before us.

> On this mountain the LORD of hosts
>   will provide for all peoples
> A feast of rich food and choice wines,
>   juicy, rich food and pure, choice wines. (25:6)

The Lord isn't going to give us army rations. He's going to give us a feast! And the Lord brings us abundance every time. At the wedding at Cana the wine ran out but he turned the water in six stone jars into wine—that's 180 gallons of wine (see John 2:1-11)! That was far more than they needed at this party.

It's not just that the Lord pulls us out of the pit. It's that the Lord divinizes us. He doesn't simply save us from damnation. He exalts us.

Or consider people who were hungry after listening to Jesus for three days. Jesus' heart was "moved with pity for the crowd" who had nothing to eat (Matthew 15:32). He was worried that perhaps they would pass out on their way home— that's how hungry they were. Jesus took the seven loaves of bread and a few fish the disciples had and from them created so much abundance that there were seven baskets full of food left over (see 15:32-39). Another time he took five loaves and two fish and there were over twelve basketsful of food left over (see 14:13-21). In Jesus' day, the people to whom he preached were never full. These were very poor people. At best, they only had just enough. And yet here Jesus gives them abundance.

When Christ comes, he brings abundance. In the Advent and Christmas seasons, we reflect on our salvation story. So how does this abundance apply to our salvation? Well, it's not just that the Lord pulls us out of the pit. It's that the Lord divinizes us. He doesn't simply save us from damnation. He exalts us. One of my favorite prayers in the whole Mass occurs during the liturgy of the Eucharist. The priest is supposed to say it quietly so unfortunately the congregation doesn't get to hear it. But this is what he says as water is poured into the wine just before the Eucharistic prayer: "Through the mingling of this water and wine, may we come to share in your divinity, as you have shared in our humanity."

The comingling of divinity and humanity by the incarnation of Christ allows us to share in his divinity. We become divine. The final coming of Christ will bring about a new heaven and a new earth. All of creation will be divinized.

So today, if you are experiencing abundance in your life, then Christmas has come early for you. You've opened your present early! If you don't feel abundance yet, then you're in Advent, both liturgically and personally. You're in an Advent season of your life where you are waiting in joyful hope and anticipation of abundance to come.

FOR REFLECTION

1. Where would you like to see some abundance in your life right now? Consider areas where you feel broken or lacking or shortchanged. God knows your needs. Talk with him frankly and ask him to abundantly provide for your needs in whatever way he wants.

2. Have you given much thought to the fact that you will share in Christ's divinity as you grow in grace? What does that mean for you? How can the promise of divinization help you to become a more faithful child of God here and now?

4

THE GRACE OF HOPE

In Isaiah, chapter 40, God asks Isaiah the prophet to speak comfort to the people, telling them to prepare a way, to make straight a highway:

> Every valley shall be lifted up,
> every mountain and hill made low. (40:4)

And what valleys does Isaiah speak about? What mountains and hills? What valleys will be filled, what mountains made low? And why do Isaiah's people need comfort? What's going on that he needs to speak words of comfort to them?

In order to understand where Isaiah is coming from, we need to go back a thousand years to the time of Moses in Egypt, because Isaiah's referring to that time in Egypt when he speaks about preparing a way. The Israelite people had been in bondage, in slavery, for four hundred years by the time Moses came around. It must have been an absolutely horrible four hundred years—not just for each and every slave, but

We learn to be hopeless when we are going through a phase of our life where no matter what we try and no matter what step we take, we find pain.

for the Israelite people as a whole. Four hundred years. They must have felt overwhelmed by hopelessness.

A psychological study from the 1960s provides insight into how the Israelites might have felt.[1] Psychologists set up a quadrant of four panels that carried a mild shockwave. They put a dog on the quadrant and allowed it to choose which of the four panels on which to sit or stand. Then the psychologists would send a shock to that panel—not hurting it so much as making it very uncomfortable so that it would want to move to one of the other panels. They found that they could shock different panels at different moments to train the dog to step from one panel to another in a pattern. At one point, however, they shocked all four panels at the same time to see what the dog would do. The dog would try one panel, then try another, then another. After a few minutes of fruitless attempts to avoid the shock, the dog would simply lie down and moan. The psychologist called this phenomenon "learned helplessness" or "learned hopelessness."

Psychologists speak about this phenomenon as being true for humans as well; we, like those dogs on the four panels when they all gave off a shock, begin to learn hopelessness. We learn to be hopeless when we are going through a phase of our life where no matter what we try and no matter what step we take, we find pain.

Because they had lost hope after four hundred years of slavery, the Israelite people in Egypt believed there was no use going any further. But when the time finally came, God told Moses to tell the people, "Your time has arrived; it's time to go, to leave slavery and enter into your Promised Land."

---

1. J. B Overmier & M. E. Seligman, "Effects of inescapable shock upon subsequent escape and avoidance responding," *Journal of Comparative and Physiological Psychology*, 63 (1967): 28–33. https://doi.org/10.1037/h0024166.

That step into the Red Sea looked like another step into hopelessness. But when they took that step, they found themselves in a place of dry land as the Red Sea parted.

The people were hesitant because they had given up, and Moses had to sort of push them to take a step of hope again. And that step of hope was into the Red Sea. It looked like another step into hopelessness. But when they took that step, they found themselves in a place of dry land as the Red Sea parted. And they were able to step forward, to take another step toward the Promised Land.

And then after that, God showed them that there would be no mountain or valley that would keep them from the Promised Land. When the people became scared in the night, God sent them a fiery column. And when they became lost in the day, he sent a cloud to lead them along the way. When they got hungry, he sent manna from the sky. When they got thirsty, he made water shoot from the rock. He was teaching the people that there would not be any obstacle that could keep them from their own Promised Land. All they had to do was forsake their learned hopelessness and take that step of hope.

The very last step toward the Promised Land was stepping into the Jordan River. And that last step was a difficult one for them. Joshua rallied them with a speech, promising that when the feet of the priests carrying the ark of the covenant entered the Jordan River, the waters would stop flowing. As we read in the Book of Joshua, all the people stepped into the Jordan River and the water receded. They then walked across dry land into the Promised Land (see Joshua 3).

All of that happened roughly a thousand years before Isaiah, and then Isaiah came along and he said, "Make straight a pathway to the Promised Land, to the Lord" (see 40:3). And he said that every valley would be filled in and every mountain and hill would be made low. He was reminding the people that

And then Jesus came and, with him, freedom from learned hopelessness.

a thousand years prior, their own people had been led out of slavery and into the Promised Land. And he was telling them that they were going to have the same experience.

Isaiah was speaking to the people of Israel who had been captured by the Babylonians. The Babylonians had carried them away to Babylonia, in present-day Iraq, and they were again in a state of learned hopelessness. Once again they were enslaved in a foreign land. As we read in Psalm 137,

> By the rivers of Babylon
>   there we sat weeping
>   when we remembered Zion.
> On the poplars in its midst
>   we hung up our harps.
> For there our captors asked us
>   For the words of a song; . . .
> But how could we sing a song of the LORD
>   in a foreign land? (137:1-4)

They had given up hope and this time it was Isaiah who said, "Every valley will be filled. Every mountain will be brought low. Nothing will keep you from your Promised Land" (see 40:4). And they took that step of faith and hope again. The Persians came along and invaded Babylon, and they set the Israelites free. The Israelites returned to their homeland. They made that journey back, but they could do so because they had forsaken their hopelessness. That's what Isaiah's prophecy is all about.

Then we have John the Baptist. God told John the Baptist to comfort his people. This time it was the Romans who were oppressing them. The Israelites didn't leave their homeland during the Roman occupation, but they started feeling hopeless again. And sad to say, it wasn't just the Romans oppressing them. The leaders of their own faith, the Pharisees, had also become a type of oppressor. The Pharisees wove a web of rules about how to be holy: stipulations that that were so complicated there was no way for the people to get past these rules and be close to God again. The Romans and the Pharisees led the people to learned hopelessness. And then God sent John the Baptist to them.

The Gospels say that John the Baptist cried, "Repent and be baptized" (see Matthew 3:1-6). We often think the word "repent" means only that we should be sorry for our sins, but it actually means something much bigger than that. The word calls for making a complete transformation of the way that we think. John the Baptist was saying, "You have to think in an entirely different way. You have to let go of all of that hopelessness and step into the river of hope. Step into the Jordan River of hope." And they did! And then Jesus came and, with him, freedom from learned hopelessness.

Fast forward to our own experience, and we can probably admit that we all have our days when we experience learned hopelessness. Every single one of us has our days when we feel that no matter where we step, there's going to be pain. No matter which way we go, we're going to encounter pain.

The grace of Advent is the grace of hope. In Advent, God is calling us to step out of our learned hopelessness and step into the river of hope. All of us, in one way or another, for one reason or another, can find ourselves in that place. Whether it's politics or religion or something happening in our own family, we all can get to that place. The Lord wants us to work on the hopelessness that we've learned over the years—from our failures, from sin, or for whatever reason. He wants each of us to step out of that dark place and into the place of hope.

FOR REFLECTION

When learned hopelessness hits, moving away from it doesn't have to be complicated. Choose one simple step you can take to step into the river of hope. Practice that every day until it becomes second nature, and then add another step. Easier said than done, but ask God to help you embrace the hope that he wants to give you.

5

WHY A BABY?

Why did God come as Savior in the form of a baby? In the spirit of Christmas, I want to think about that question. God wanted to save the world, and he chose to save the world by coming as a baby. God is all-powerful, so he could have chosen so many different ways to accomplish our salvation. I have to admit, I think he made a strange choice. He could have come as one of my favorite superhero characters, Iron Man. As Iron Man he could have used all that great technology and just kind of wiped away all of the sin of the world. Or he could have come as Spider-Man and danced around on those webs and taken care of the world that way. Or maybe, like the Flash, he could have run around the world and healed everybody quickly.

God could have come in all kinds of ways. He could have come as a king in a castle or as the president of the United States or as a movie star. Or he could have come as the wealthiest person in the world and given everybody gifts.

Consider: who were the first people to hear about the baby Jesus, besides Mary and Joseph, after he was born? The shepherds.

So why would God choose to save the world as a little baby? Babies aren't very impressive. They don't do much—they pretty much just lie there and cry and poop. It's a weird choice, in my opinion. And not only that, he came as a very poor baby when he could have been born into a wealthy family. More than that, he came as a poor baby who had to sleep with the farm animals. So we have to ask, *Why did he come as a poor baby who slept with the farm animals?*

Stop for a minute and think about that question in the context of your own experience. Maybe this has happened to you. Imagine that you are a child at the playground. You see some of your friends—people you really like—over on the other side of the playground. They're talking and laughing together, but when you walk over and say, "Hey, what's going on?" they all go silent and say, "Oh, nothing." The same thing can happen to us as adults, in one way or another, maybe at a party or at the office. And when it happens, how does that make us feel? Left out. Nobody likes to feel excluded.

Now let's take this feeling of being left out and consider it not only in light of Jesus' entry into the world as a helpless baby, but also in his revelation to the most left-out people of his time.

Consider: who were the first people to hear about the baby Jesus, besides Mary and Joseph, after he was born? The shepherds. They were the first ones to receive the news. What do you think their socioeconomic status was? Do you think they were high up? That they were greatly respected? In people's minds, shepherds were at the very bottom of the pile. Nobody really paid much attention to them. They were poor, and they took care of the sheep out in the pasture.

Whenever there was a party, they had to stay out in the field with the sheep. If you had to name one group of people in Jesus' day who were left out of everything, it would have been the shepherds. They even had to sleep outside in the field with the animals.

And there we have a hint as to why God chose to be a poor baby who had to sleep with the animals. Our Good Shepherd, Jesus, came as a poor baby born among the animals because he wanted to go first to the ones who were most left out: the shepherds.

That tells us a lot about Jesus. When Jesus came to the Earth, he came to help those who felt left out and he started with the group that was most left out: the shepherds. And then, as he grew up, he went to all the other outcasts.

For all of us, whenever we feel left out, we can be assured that God is with us in that moment because that's how he himself started—by choosing to be with the people who were left out.

That's the whole story of Christmas. That's the whole reason why God came to the Earth: to be with us, to save us, to never leave us out.

FOR REFLECTION

1. It hurts to be left out, but it happens to everyone. When it happens to you, take a moment to turn to Jesus and remind you of his presence with you. If you carry any of those times as an unresolved burden, look for ways to overcome your pain and rejoice in the life God has given you.

2. Have you ever deliberately left someone out or ignored them? Consider how you can make amends for that slight. It's never too late to apologize for even long-ago wrongs we have done to other people.

6

GAUDETE! REJOICE ALWAYS!

"Rejoice in the Lord always" (Philippians 4:4). This is St. Paul's command to us in the Bible. Paul leans on it when he continues: "I shall say it again: rejoice!" (4:4).

We all want to be good Christians. We read through the Bible. We try to follow everything Christ calls us to do. We take these commands very seriously. Many of them are difficult and sobering and even hard to hear, such as taking up our crosses (see Matthew 16:24) or being watchful and alert (see 1 Peter 5:8; Ephesians 6:18; 1 Thessalonians 5:6).

But we don't always take as seriously this command to rejoice always. Perhaps we don't follow this command because it sounds a little impossible, doesn't it? Rejoice always? How can we possibly rejoice always? How could you be serious, St. Paul, telling us that we should always be joyful?

It depends on what we mean by Christian joy. Christian joy is not the same thing as happiness. Happiness is a sort of giddy emotion we experience when the circumstances are fortunate for us. That's what happiness is. If you give me a

We know that Christ will come!
And so we're joyful.

bowl of my favorite ice cream, I'm going to be happy. And how long will that happiness last? You know the answer: it'll last as long as the ice cream lasts. That's happiness. Joy is something altogether different. Joy is a choice or a disposition toward life, regardless of the circumstances. Joy is making a choice to have a certain disposition in life.

Let me give you an analogy. Let's say your favorite football team is (of course!) the New Orleans Saints. Let's say you love the Saints and you love watching their games. But you can't watch the game this weekend, so you set your television to record it. But before you get a chance to watch it, you hear what happened. You hear that they got beat up throughout the game. It was just terrible. They kept messing up and they looked terrible against the opponent. But at the very end of the game, they came through in the last seconds and won.

Let's say you heard all of that and then you press "play" and start watching the game. When you see one of those terrible plays, are you going to be devastated? No, because you know the end of the game. That's like the Christian disposition of joy. Bad things happen to us in the second quarter and the third quarter, but we know what's going to happen in the fourth quarter of the game. We know that Christ will come! And so we're joyful. We have Christian joy.

There's a silly story that also offers insight into the concept of Christian joy. A mom and dad thought their son was too happy—they wanted him to be more sober, to know how hard life is. So they took him to a wacky psychologist who said, "I know how to put a bit of sobriety in him." He filled a room full of manure and he put the child in this room. Then he said, "Let's leave him there for a little while and let him absorb the

Jesus is coming soon! That's why we have this disposition that doesn't change regardless of our circumstances.

smell of this terrible manure so he'll know that life isn't all sun and flowers and balloons."

They left him in there a few minutes and then went in only to find he was happier than ever. He was digging through the manure. And they asked him, "Son, why are you digging through the manure?" And the boy replied, "Well, there's got to be a pony in here somewhere!"

That's Christian joy.

If we look at our world from a certain disposition, we can all say we have a room full of manure. Look at the politics tearing away at our nation. Look at the conflicts in the world. We don't even need to go that far, do we? In fact, we can look right in our own families and at our friends and say, "We have a room full of manure here!" But a Christian will say, "There's a pony in here somewhere." In other words, we have Jesus Christ. And Jesus is coming. He's coming soon! And that's why we're joyful. That's why we have this disposition that doesn't change regardless of our circumstances.

But what if, instead of acknowledging the pony, we more often find ourselves contemplating the manure? John the Baptist had something to say about that attitude. The Baptist said that when Christ comes, he's going to bring his winnowing fan to winnow out the chaff from the wheat (see Matthew 3:12). What is a winnowing fan? There are different kinds, but there's one that looks sort of like a colander—you pour the wheat onto it, shake it, and the chaff sort of floats away into the air and the wheat falls down into your bowl. That's what happens when you winnow.

So what's the chaff, then, that Christ wants to winnow out? What's the chaff weighing down our joy? The chaff is sarcasm, cynicism, judgmentalism, pessimism, divisiveness. That's the chaff. What's the wheat? It's faith, hope, love, a spirit of community, and unity. That's the wheat. If we are doing the work of Christ, we're going to winnow out all that chaff—not because we aren't acknowledging how hard the world is, but because we know that we have a Savior and that everything is going to be okay.

Of all that wheat—faith, hope, and love—I want to focus on hope because hope is the grace that we pray for in Advent, and especially on Gaudete (Rejoice) Sunday, the third Sunday of Advent. In Advent, especially as the season progresses, we see the essential connection between joy and hope. In short, we can rejoice because we have hope.

Joyful hope is different from optimism. Optimism says, "Everything's going to be okay." Hope says, "Everything is not going to be okay, but Christ is going to be with me, so I'm going to be okay. And Christ is going to be with you, too. So you're going to be okay, too." That's hope. That's the disposition that we have when we "rejoice . . . always," as St. Paul told us to do (Philippians 4:4). He wrote those words from prison, by the way. But rejoicing always takes a lot of work, doesn't it? It's not so easy. Someone once said that happiness is no laughing matter. Well, hope is no laughing matter. Christian joy is no laughing matter. We have to actually work at it.

We must do all we can to not "quench the Spirit" (1 Thessalonians 5:19), to not snuff out the Spirit, the flame of the Spirit of God. Think of scouts learning how to light a flame on a cold winter night with a hard wind blowing. They light a tiny flame and then they feed it very gently, very carefully, until they can build it up. It takes work. And it takes work to keep this sort of joyful hope—the flame of joyful hope—alive. That's the work of the Christian. There's a Christian organization with the tagline "Hope is sweaty." It sure is. We have to work at it in order to keep that flame of hope alive in our hearts.

In the First Letter of Peter we read: "Always be ready to provide an explanation to anyone who asks you for a reason for your hope" (3:15). St. Peter knew that if you and I have this joyful hope in the midst of a world full of manure, we're going to be attacked. How dare you be joyful in the midst of all of this pain and misery? We have to be ready to defend our hope. And if we defend it well, we'll spread hope to others.

There are two things we need to pray and work towards. One is having hope. The other is defending that hope so it spreads to the rest of the world. That's what we do as Christians. And if we're going to do this hard work, we need to get our calories in. We need to get some protein in us. And how do we do that? We come to Christ, and we consume the Host.

At the risk of spoiling Christmas for you, I'm going to tell you that Jesus is born in a manger. The word manger has its roots in Latin (*mandere*, to chew) and old French (*mangier*, to eat) and applies here as the place where animals eat. In Cajun French, we use this word all the time: "mangez." Anytime we put a great feast out on the table we say, "Mangez!" "Eat!" Jesus was born in a manger, the place where the farm animals eat. Where is our manger? Where do we come to be fed? We come to the altar. We feed from Christ, born in the manger, and so we have hope, we have joy.

We know what happens in the fourth quarter, just as we know there's a pony inside that room of manure. And so we live with joyful hope, ready to defend it for anyone who asks for an explanation.

FOR REFLECTION

1. Hope is at the core of who we are as Christians—all our fears are laid to rest with the coming of Christ. How can you fan the flame of hope in your life, particularly in an area where you feel little hope?

2. Does rejoicing come naturally to you or are you more of a glass-half-empty kind of person? Take time to think about how cynicism and negativity affect not only you but also those around you. Resolve during this Advent to explore the roots of your attitude and find ways to develop a more Christian outlook on life.

7

THE GRACE OF
ANTICIPATION

My parish has a Catholic elementary school. Recently one of the teachers asked the kids, "What's your favorite day of the week?" I thought that the kids would answer Saturday—because this is the day that they're off, they're free. But they said Friday was their favorite day. When the teacher asked why, she discovered it was because they spent all day Friday in anticipation of the weekend. Even though they were still in a "work day," they spent Friday in anticipation, and that actually brought them even more joy than the day off itself.

I love this choice the kids made because, in a way, it shows us what Advent is about. Advent is sort of our "Friday." It's the day before the "great day"—the moment Christ is present in the Incarnation. So Advent can actually be a time of tremendous joy for us, and I think the Lord wants us to be joyful during Advent. Anticipation can be a joyful state. Advent has that same dark, violet color that Lent has, but for a different

We should pray about this:
how is Christ present to me now
and yet still in the womb?

reason. We're not quite so sober and somber as we were in Lent, because we are in joyful anticipation.

But this Advent anticipation is different from, say, waiting for an out-of-town guest to come to your house at Christmas. Let's say that my brother Eric is coming to my house for Christmas. Well, he isn't here yet, so there is an absence of my brother Eric. The "advent" period before my out-of-town brother comes to town is a time of "no presence" of Eric. But that's not what the Advent of Christ is like because Christ is actually present in Advent.

And that's where a misconception can take hold: to think of Advent as a time when we reflect on not having Christ, and then at Christmas, we have Christ. Instead, we know that Christ is fully present in Advent because he came into the world over two thousand years ago and has been with us ever since. And yet in Advent how is Christ fully present? Christ is present in gestation, in the womb. He is here with us, but in this state of gestation.

When we reflect on Advent and what the Lord might want us to pray about and what graces we might receive, we should pray about this: how is Christ present to me now and yet still in the womb? How am I still in the place of anticipation but still in his presence? So much is happening all around us as we anticipate his arrival, and yet Christ is present now.

So although he is already present, Christ calls us, in Advent, to experience him as present in the spirit of gestation. What would it mean for Christ to be in gestation for us right at this moment? Think of it this way: God the Father wants to send his Son to be present to all people and he is in search of another womb. In other words, he is in search of those who can bring his Son into the world. And so the question is, Is your "womb" available? Are you ready to bear Christ for the world this year? Are you ready to be like Mary this year? How can you "give birth" to Christ, for others, in the world today?

FOR REFLECTION

What does the idea of "gestating" Christ mean for you as you consider your call to bring Christ to those around you? This Advent, pray about what tasks he has given you in your daily life. How can this time of gestation better equip you to do those essential but everyday tasks?

8

AN EMPTY SPACE

It seems that among the many qualities of Mary that God the Father liked was her chastity. I can say a thing or two about chastity because I've been living chastely for my entire adult life. Many years ago, Fr. Henri Nouwen wrote one of my favorite spiritual reflections on the topic, for people with the vow of chastity.[1] Fr. Nouwen said that that his favorite thing about chastity from a spiritual perspective is that when we take the vow of chastity, we create an empty space for God to fill. Chastity is about creating an empty space for God to fill—creating a sort of hole inside your heart that only God is able to fill.

I've always really loved that image. He goes further and uses the metaphor of an enormous church. When you think about a church and you start talking about the church, you're usually talking about the walls, the marble floor, the ceiling. But a church is mostly vast open space—we actually love that about a church. Because in our hearts, even underneath the

---

1. Henri Nouwen, *Clowning in Rome: Reflections on Solitude, Celibacy, Prayer, and Contemplation* (New York: Random House, 2013), 36.

We love vast open space because
we know that it's a space for our vast
God to fill.

level of consciousness, we know that it's a space for our vast God to fill.

We can contrast this with another building: the inn of the Christmas story. It was too cluttered and full to let in even a new baby. The question for us is: Are we the open space that can be filled with a new manifestation of God? Or are our lives this Advent season so cluttered that we cannot squeeze even a tiny new manifestation of God into our lives? Let's pray that we might have an open space in our hearts and on our calendars and within our entire lives—a space in which a new manifestation of God can be born.

FOR REFLECTION

1. This Advent season, think about and pray for priests, religious, and single people who have chosen to be chaste so they might create space for God within. Make space in your own heart and life for them, and find ways to encourage and support them.

2. Regardless of your state of life, might you learn from the "open space" of chastity? Might you create and open space within your heart and within your life in order for God to come and fill it with his presence?

3. All of us, regardless of our state in life, can throw open our lives to God. Do you fear what might happen if you do that or are you ready for whatever might come? Ask God to lead you to an even greater generosity of spirit, regardless, so that he can touch more lives, including your own.

9

GABRIEL, STILL SEARCHING TODAY

I've wanted to be a priest ever since I was a little boy, but in my eighteenth year, on a Jesuit retreat weekend, the deal was finally sealed. An elderly Jesuit—a really good faithful priest who had lived his whole life in service as a Jesuit priest—gave the talks for the retreat. And I was so moved by this man that I decided this is what I wanted to do. I remember so well a moment in the retreat when he became personal and said, "Looking over my long life as a Jesuit priest, nowadays when I lift up the Host at Mass and I say those awesome words 'This is my body,' I sometimes hear my heart say to Jesus at the same time, 'It's my body, too, Lord.' And when I lift up the chalice and I say those awesome words 'This is my blood, given up for you,' I find myself saying to the Lord, 'This is my blood, too.'"

I wanted to be this man. I wanted to come to the end of my life and be able to say, "It's my body, too. It's my blood, sweat, and tears, too."

We, too, are a part of that salvation story. We are main characters in the scene at the creche.

Poetically speaking, we could say that Mary was the first priest, because Mary was the first to bring the real presence of Christ to the world. She was the first to literally bring the body and blood of Christ to the world. And it all started with her body, didn't it? It all started with her giving up her body thirty-some years before her son, Jesus, gave his in the Passion. She said the equivalent, at the Annunciation, to God through Gabriel: "Take this. This is my body given up for the salvation of the world" (see Luke 1:38). These words capture what is so beautiful about the story of the Incarnation.

The Incarnation would be beautiful if it were simply about the fact that God chose to come and enflesh himself and give that body away for the salvation of the world. That would be beautiful enough, but God also chose to let us play a role in that salvation story. We, too, are a part of that salvation story. We are main characters in the scene at the creche. We are an important part of our own salvation story and even more than that, we are an important part of each other's salvation story. Your salvation is intricately connected to my saying "yes" to God's call, and my salvation is intricately connected to your saying "yes" to your call.

When I preside at Mass, the congregation is able to receive Jesus Christ in the Eucharist because years ago I said to God on my ordination day, "Take this. This is my body given up for you." In order for a dad to be the Christian dad that God calls him to be, he had to say to his wife on their wedding day, "Take this. This is my body." For a mom to be the Christian mom that she's called to be, on her wedding day she had to say to her husband, "Take this, this is my body." Every teacher, every nurse, every bus driver, every maintenance worker—for each of us, in whatever way God has called us to bring Jesus to the world—we must say, as Mary said, as Jesus said, "Take this, this is my body given up for you."

In Advent, we celebrate three comings of Christ. The first coming of Christ was two thousand years ago when he came as a baby boy in the manger. The final coming of Christ is at the end of time. But it's the middle coming of Christ—the in-between coming of Christ—that is just as important today. Christ wants to come again in this year, and Gabriel is roaming the Earth looking for those who, like Mary, will say, "Take this, this is my body given up for the salvation of the world."

FOR REFLECTION

1. What does it mean, on a daily basis, in small and big ways, for someone to lay down their life? What does it mean for you to do so for others?

2. Maybe, during this Advent, you're waiting for God to make known to you his calling for your life. Whether you're waiting to know your life vocation or something as practical as whether or not to move or change jobs, confirm in your heart that in whatever you do, you want to lay down your life for God's purposes.

10

THE GRACE OF YOUR FIAT

F iat. This is what we call Mary's yes when the angel Gabriel came to her. Fiat is a Greek word that literally means "Let it be as you wish." And here it refers to the moment in Scripture when Mary answers the angel Gabriel, "May it be done to me according to your word" (Luke 1:38).

When I was younger and a little less mature in the spiritual life, I thought of Mary as a very fragile and maybe even weak and docile teenage girl who just sort of went along with whatever God was asking her to do. But if you look at the roots of that word "fiat," it gives us an insight into who Mary really was.

The word "fiat" is used to indicate a decree issued by royalty. When someone such as a king or a queen issues a fiat, they are issuing a declaration and also a command. They are declaring that a world-changing event is about to happen, and they are commanding that the world accept this event. So for example, when Constantine in the fourth century AD decided that Christianity would be the world religion, he issued a fiat, basically the same thing as an edict.

God is waiting for us to say,
"Let it be done. I will bring Christ
into the world."

If we apply this to Mary, what this means is that Mary is not a docile teenage girl just going along with what God is saying. She is issuing a fiat. She is a queen, and she's making a proclamation: "Let it be done just as God has proclaimed." Mary is fully in control of her choice because God has given her the choice of yes or no. And she in fact is saying, "Yes, let it be." She's issuing her edict, her fiat.

As far as I know, apart from Mary's usage, the word fiat appears in the Bible in only one other place. In Genesis 1, God says, "Let there be light" (1:3). "Fiat luz." God, as king of the universe, is saying, "Let there be light." He is proclaiming and commanding light. Mary, issuing her fiat, is issuing it as a queen: "Let it be done."

So what does this have to do with us? Well, I think that God is waiting for our fiat. God wants to send his Son into the world and make Christ incarnate once again this year. When we think of the season of Advent, we usually think of ourselves as waiting on God. We're waiting for God to do God's great act of the Incarnation. That's completely true, of course. But there's another way of looking at this: God is actually waiting on us. What is he waiting for us to do? He's waiting for us to follow in Mary's footsteps—to issue our edict, our fiat. God is waiting for us to say, "Let it be done. I will bring Christ into the world. I will bear Christ for God into the world today."

I'd like to close with a story. I was a novice director for many years. One of the great joys and privileges of this role was leading novices in a thirty-day silent retreat using the Spiritual Exercises of St. Ignatius Loyola. As you probably know, the Spiritual Exercises draw the retreatant prayerfully and powerfully into each moment of the Gospels. On one of these retreats, I was with a novice who was an extreme extrovert. He just talked nonstop. One day, he was praying about the Annunciation—about Gabriel coming to Mary and Mary giving her fiat. As he was praying over this passage, imagining the scene, he was so moved that he was just talking to God nonstop. He was saying, "Oh God, isn't this wonderful? I love this scene and Mary looks so beautiful." Essentially he was giving a stream-of-consciousness commentary on the scene. But at that moment, he distinctly heard God the Father say, "Shhh. This is my favorite part." God the Father shushed my wonderful novice and told him, "This is my favorite part."

This is our moment. God is coming to us and asking, "Will you bear Christ for the world? Will you issue your own fiat"? Will we say yes? This is God's favorite part, and he is waiting with bated breath to hear our answer.

FOR REFLECTION

1. Just as Mary freely said yes to God, you can say yes as well, although you might sometimes find yourself holding back. If that's the case, ask the Holy Spirit to help you uncover the things that stand in the way of your "yes" and then lead you on a path to a full and free fiat.

2. Some of our fiats are life-changing, of course, but most simply move us along a lifelong road to greater holiness. Choose two or three daily, ordinary demands you experience in your life, and commit yourself to saying yes to a merciful, loving response in those circumstances.

Afterword

Jesus, God Incarnate,

I rejoice in anticipation of the abundant grace of your coming.

May I search for your coming among the small, the weak, and the outcast.

But may I also search for your newborn presence within my own spiritual womb.

I empty myself in order to create a space for you to be born within me.

Like Mary, I say, "Fiat—let it be," that I, too, may bear your presence to the world.

May your coming as a vulnerable baby bring peace between the lion and lamb, beginning within me.

May your light dispel my darkness and hopelessness—and the world's, too.

Fiat! May it be done!

Amen.

Also by Fr. Mark Thibodeaux

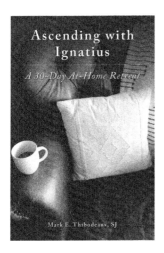

Ascending with Ignatius
A 30-Day At-Home Retreat

Deepen your faith life with this at-home retreat! Mark E. Thibodeaux, SJ, combines his Louisiana storytelling, his knowledge of the Spiritual Exercises of St. Ignatius, and his gifts as a spiritual director to create an at-home retreat that is a journey of transformation. Experience God's presence in a deeper way, and encounter God's personal love for you as you follow along with this book over thirty days.

Order today at Amazon or bookstore.wau.org.

theWORD
among us®

The Word Among Us publishes a monthly devotional magazine, books, Bible studies, and pamphlets that help Catholics grow in their faith.

To learn more about who we are and what we publish, visit www.wau.org. There you will find a variety of Catholic resources that will help you grow in your faith.

Your review makes a difference! If you enjoyed this book, please consider sharing your review on Amazon using the QR code below.

Embrace His Word
Listen to God . . .

www.wau.org

Printed in Great Britain
by Amazon

51213979R00046